Caring for the Earth

Let's Save Water!

by Sara E. Nelson

Consulting Editor: Gail Saunders-Smith, PhD

Consultant: Kate M. Krebs
Executive Director, National Recycling Coalition, Inc.

Capstone
press®
Mankato, Minnesota

Pebble Books are published by Capstone Press,
151 Good Counsel Drive, P.O. Box 669, Mankato, Minnesota 56002.
www.capstonepress.com

1 2 3 4 5 6 11 10 09 08 07 06

Library of Congress Cataloging-in-Publication Data
Nelson, Sara Elizabeth.
    Let's save water! / by Sara E. Nelson.
    p. cm.—(Pebble Books. Caring for the earth)
    Summary: "Simple text and photographs describe why it's important to save
water and simple ways children can save water"—Provided by publisher.
    Includes bibliographical references and index.
    ISBN-13: 978-0-7368-6322-3 (hardcover)
    ISBN-10: 0-7368-6322-2 (hardcover)
    1. Water conservation—Juvenile literature. 2. Water—Pollution—Juvenile
literature. I. Title. II. Series.
TD388.N45 2007
333.91'16—dc22   2006005054

Note to Parents and Teachers

The Caring for the Earth set supports national science standards
related to conservation and environmental change. This book
describes and illustrates ways children can conserve water. The
images support early readers in understanding the text. The
repetition of words and phrases helps early readers learn new
words. This book also introduces early readers to subject-specific
vocabulary words, which are defined in the Glossary section. Early
readers may need assistance to read some words and to use the
Table of Contents, Glossary, Read More, Internet Sites, and Index
sections of the book.

Table of Contents

We Need Water

People, plants, and
animals use water
to grow and live.

Earth has a lot of water.
But only a little bit
is safe for people to use.

Water Problems

Our water is in danger.
People waste water
by using too much.

People pollute water.
They put garbage
in rivers and lakes.

Help Save Water

Emma saves water.
She turns off the faucet
when she brushes
her teeth.

Josh takes a quick shower instead of a bath.
He uses less water.

Maria fills the dishwasher full before she starts it. She saves water.

18

Emily and her friends keep water clean. They pick up garbage near lakes and oceans.

When you save water,
you help the Earth
stay healthy.
Then we all can enjoy
the water we need.

Glossary

faucet—something you use to turn water on and off

garbage—items you throw away because you do not need or want them anymore

pollute—to make dirty or unsafe

waste—to use something foolishly or carelessly; when you leave the faucet on while you brush your teeth, unused water goes down the drain; this is wasteful.

Read More

Ballard, Carol. *How We Use Water.* Raintree Perspectives. Chicago: Raintree, 2005.

Nelson, Robin. *Water.* First Step Nonfiction. Minneapolis: Lerner, 2005.

Internet Sites

FactHound offers a safe, fun way to find Internet sites related to this book. All of the sites on FactHound have been researched by our staff.

Here's how:

1. Visit *www.facthound.com*
2. Choose your grade level.
3. Type in this book ID **0736863222** for age-appropriate sites. You may also browse subjects by clicking on letters, or by clicking on pictures and words.
4. Click on the **Fetch It** button.

FactHound will fetch the best sites for you!

Index

Word Count: 121
Grade: 1
Early-Intervention Level: 14

Editorial Credits
Mari Schuh, editor; Juliette Peters, designer; Wanda Winch, photo researcher;
    Scott Thoms, photo editor

Photo Credits
Capstone Press/Karon Dubke, cover
Getty Images Inc./The Image Bank/Mike Brinson, 20; Photographer's Choice/
    Darrell Gulin, 4
Photodisc/John A. Rizzo, 8
PhotoEdit Inc./David Young-Wolff, 18; Michael Newman, 12; Myrleen Ferguson
    Cate, 16; Tony Freeman, 14
Shutterstock/Jim Jurica, 10; Oleg Kozlov, Sophy Kozlova, 6; Rudolf Georg, 1